Beautiful Day

poems

J. R. Solonche

DEERBROOK EDITIONS

PUBLISHED BY
Deerbrook Editions
P.O. Box 542
Cumberland ME 04021
www.deerbrookeditions.com
issuu.com/deerbrookeditions

FIRST EDITION

ISBN: 978-0-9904287-2-5

Book design by Jeffrey Haste
Cover by Jeffrey Haste

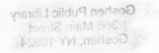

1/20

Acknowledgments

Thanks to the editors of the following periodicals in which these poems, some in a slightly different form and/or with a different title, first appeared.

Atlanta Review: *To My Beard*
Barrow Street: *Banks*
Blood Lotus: *When You Hit the Stones*
Bryant Literary Review: *Doing Seventy on the Highway*
Centrifugal Eye: *Glass Ghazal*
Chronogram: *Beauty*
Columbia Review: *When I Heard on the Radio*
Contemporary American Voices: *The Path*
DMQ Review: *Why I Stopped Going to the Chiropractor*
Hampden-Sydney Poetry Review: *Pomegranate*
Mudlark: An Electronic Journal of Poerty & Poetics: *Horse Ghazal, Cow Ghazal, Wine Ghazal, Sky Ghazal*
Natural Bridge: *House Ghazal*
Poet & Critic: *Slug, I Read a Poem Today about a Spider*
Rattle: *A Dialogue with My Daughter Through the Window of Her Dollhouse*
Review Americana: *To the Deaf Student in My Poetry Class before I Play a Recording of Dylan Thomas*
Salmagundi: *Smoking*
Skidrow Penthouse: *Pocket Watch*
Slant: *To My Favorite Corduroy Jacket*
Umbrella: *Beautiful Day*
Words on Paper: *The Author Mural above the Coffee Bar at Barnes & Noble*

Contents

For Joan and Emily

PART I

Pomegranate

When I was eleven or twelve,
I was easy to make fun of.
I was tall and comically thin.
I wore glasses, thick ones that made
my eyes protrude like a frog's eyes.
I had buckteeth and a big nose.
On rainy or near-rainy days,
I had to wear rubber overshoes.
I was called "four-eyes" most often,
I was called "the frog-face" sometimes,
and once or twice "four-eyes frog-face."
Once some older kids following
me home, punched me hard in the back.
I heard one say to the others,
"Hey guys, look, four-eyes can take it."
Three days later Mrs. Pogrow
told the class to bring in something
special. Because I couldn't think
of anything, my mother put
a pomegranate in a brown
bag and told me it was the real
apple that Adam and Eve ate
in the Garden of Eden. On
my way to school, I took it out
to look at. It was ruby-red
and heavy and hard as granite.
I thought that's how it got its name.
I ran the remaining four blocks,
busting to set the record straight
about Genesis and the fruit
all of the Bronx had gotten wrong.
Arriving at the playground gate,
I saw the puncher and his friends
waiting for me, smiling those small,
feared, hated smiles. I paused. And then,
my secret weapon gripped fiercely
in my hand, I charged in. I was
Samson slaying the Philistines

with jawbone of pomegranate,
I was Thor swinging his magic
pomegranate hammer, I was
Superman punching bad guys flat
with steely pomegranate fist.
So lightning bolts flashed from frog eyes,
thunderbolts boomed from bony arm.
It was the only time they did.

I Often Walk to the End of The Road

I often walk to the end of the road
to look at the abandoned farm.
I like to look at the field
as it goes back to wilderness again.
I like to look at the grass grow
higher and thicker around the barn,
embrace it with its hairy arms
as though welcoming back the wood.
I like to look at the barn turn more
and more gray. It sags in the middle.
It reminds me of the last old horse
that years ago stood as still as a barn.
I like to watch the earth at work.
So slowly, so patiently, so deliberately
the earth works. I like to watch
the earth turn the blue farm machines
to brown rust, turn the red farm
machines to brown rust, turn
the green farm machines to brown rust.
I like to look at her work with metal,
which is mortal like us. "No hurry,"
the earth smiles at me as I watch
her work. How patient she is
with them, with the hay wain,
with the tractor, with the plow.
"No hurry," she smiles. "No hurry."

Mailbox

My neighbor's mailbox has a broken jaw.
It hangs there. It can't be closed.
Which means when I pass by,
I can see if there's mail in it or not.
Most of the time there isn't.
When there is, it's one or two envelopes.
White or blue. Flat. They look like bills.
Never a newspaper. Never even a catalog.
I envy him. But I also feel sorry for him.
I keep telling myself I'll write him a letter.
Just so he'd get something other than
those flat blue and white envelopes.
But I never do. What would I write?
Dear neighbor, This is just a note so you
could get something other than those blue
and white envelopes. Sincerely, Your
neighbor. I think I'll just keep doing
what I've been doing all these years.
Return his broken wave with my broken wave.

When I Heard on the Radio

When I heard on the radio
that the student who was asked
by the college interviewer, "If
you could be an inanimate
object, what would you choose?"
had answered, "A revolver,"
I first thought of Emily Dickinson's
My life had stood a loaded gun,
and then I thought how I would
have answered. "A telescope,"
I said out loud, to no one, for I was
alone in the car driving home.
"A telescope is both phallic and
an instrument for advancing man's
knowledge," I said, once again out
loud, offering the reasons for my choice.
At home, I asked my wife, "If you
could be an inanimate object, what
would you choose?" "A basket,"
she answered, which surprised me
because my wife is an accomplished
classical pianist, and I was sure she
would answer, "A piano." At night,
in bed, in the dark, we lay next to one
another, my telescopic hand in the
basket of her palm and fingers,
the only sound the clicking of an
insect's wings against the window
screen, like an empty revolver.

The End of History

It was December seventh.
I asked them if they knew the significance of the date.
One said the semester's almost over.
Another said 18 shopping days 'til Christmas.
A third said it's your birthday.
No, I said. No, I said. No, I said.
Then a fourth one said it's Pearl Harbor.
Yes, I said.
The same one said when the kamikazes sank our ships.
No, I said.
There were no kamikazes at Pearl Harbor, I said
They weren't used until later, when Japan was losing, I said.
When they were almost all out of pilots and planes, I said.
The same one said then how did they sink our ships?
The same one said if they didn't crash their planes into them?
I drew a cartoon aircraft carrier on the board.
I drew cartoon dive bombers flying from the cartoon ship to a cartoon
Hawaii.
I drew cartoon torpedo planes flying to the cartoon Hawaii.
I drew cartoon bombs falling on our cartoon ships.
I drew cartoon torpedoes blowing up our cartoon ships.
This is how, I said.
So this is how history ends.
So that bastard Bush was right.
Nine-eleven really did change everything.

I Read a Poem Today about a Spider

I read a poem today about a spider,
who, smaller than an ant, wasn't worth killing,
and all day I've thought a lot about that spider
and the size a spider ought to be to be worth

killing, whether a spider ought to be the same
size as an ant or whether it ought to be bigger
than an ant to be worth killing, and if so
how much bigger than an ant a spider

ought to be, twice as big, five times, ten,
and I thought that someone really ought
to have an answer to this question for
it is a question worth someone's time,

some scientist, some molecular biologist
with advanced degrees in molecular biology,
or some theologian with advanced degrees
in theology and comparative religion,

or some physicist of subatomic physics,
surely ought to know the precise size,
the exact calculation, the absolute zero of worth,
the cause and effect, the quantum of killing.

Why I Stopped Going to the Chiropractor

My cat is sleeping upside-down.
She is dreaming.
I know what she is dreaming of.
The scientists have told us.
She is dreaming of hunting and grooming.
I could have told the scientists that.
I sleep upside-down when I sleep.
That's impossible.
The chiropractor told me that.
I know what I dream of.
I dream of hunting and grooming in my own way.
I know my dreams do not mean anything.
The scientists told us that.
I believe them.
My dreams mean what my cat's dreams mean.
I could have told them that dreams are one part of the brain
trying to make sense of another part of the brain.
This is the same as being awake.
Cats know that.
When I die, I want to be cremated.
If I should change my mind between now and then, do this.
Bury me standing up.
Even if the undertaker says it is impossible.

The World Through the Glass Wall of the Cardiology Pavillion

It is almost the real world.
Mostly sky, almost as blue as it really is.

A line of clouds toward the bottom, almost as white as they really are.
A foreground of trees almost as green as they really are.

And visible through the gaps,
almost as autonomic, almost as unconscious, almost as natural,

a stream of cars like the blood cells in the artery of your arm.
The real world.

Such a curious place.
Everyday the mirrored wall of your dreams dissolves.

Everyday it resolves into the glass wall of your world awake.
The real world.

Almost as real as the world as it is.
Almost as real as the dream of the real blood in your real heart.

The Path

A spring-like day in Autumn.
November tries warmth on
and it fits. On the common,
a flag football game.

A girlfriend watches
her small-time hero
run his predetermined zero
into the green patches.

I circle around the players,
shift my bag from hand to hand.
They do not understand
what the past is. The future,

too, is a mystery to them.
To these, time is nothing.
To me, everything.
They ride the pendulum.

I count each swing,
perpetually, back and forth.
I hasten along the arcing path
and look up without looking.

To know what will happen
never makes what happens easier.
The ash leaves seek one another
on the ground, to form again,

in the path's curve, an ash tree,
and on the lawn of Morrison Hall
the brown and red leaves fall,
and in front of the library

maples get lost in light.
The faces blur into one face,
and the names, without a trace,
disappear overnight.

I see myself in the glass
of the door, a shadow, hurled
through the zero of the world.
Harmless, I pass

in, to disengage,
to read the maples lost
in light, to read the frost
coming on, to read a page

or two, to read the man
looking back in the glass
like a book I read once,
and since have forgotten.

West Points Cadets on a Helicopter Training Exercise Fly Over My House

Before I saw them rise over the trees,
I heard the roar of the rotors.
This is what frightened them during
that war, this sound, not so much thunder

as the sky itself shaking loose
from the earth, and about to fall.
Then I saw their hideous excuse
for shape, black, sharp, exoskeletal,

their plexiglass faces sucking breaths
of sun, and I felt what they felt:
not merely the fear of death
but the horror of that fear made explicit

in the ugliest sleep of the ugliest night.
I knew in these machines were citizens
of my country innocent of any fight.
I waved to them. Then I shot them down.

Depressed

I get up from
the rocking chair,
which then
rocks thirty-four

times by itself.
The lights, diagonally
in the room,
crisscross me.

I cast two shadows.
He was right.
One should not
write poems at night.

The clock makes
a face at me.
I make a face back.
I have no dignity.

Where is the train?
And the wan whistle?
I need to hear it,
the long rumble

of the wheels
on the tracks
like the works
of a million breaking clocks.

I need to hear
the long groan
through the dark
of the freight train.

I am depressed.
So I need to hear
now a sad music.
If not sad, then sadder

than this. No train
tonight. No long,
low, dark moan
through the dark.

More depressed,
I go down to bed.
An iron silence
rusts in my head.

Doing Seventy on the Highway

Doing seventy on the highway,
I look over at my wife.
She is sleeping.
Her head is tilted against
the subtle curve of window.
In my mirrors,
eighteen-wheelers loom up
out of nowhere,
tailgate for a moment,
then spit their headlights and pass,
each one a thunderstorm
splitting the horizon in front of me.
White thunderstorm.
Red thunderstorm.
Yellow thunderstorm.
I consider doing seventy-five.
I don't. Instead I look back at my daughter.
She is sleeping.
Her head is dropped on her chest.
I reach behind and push her chin up.
Thus far this summer
this is summer's finest day.
The sky is blue pure through.
On the hood of my car,
the sun does a golden dance.
Tell me, Sol Invictus,
what the speed of darkness is.
I have to go faster.

A Dialogue with My Daughter through the Window of Her Doll house

"The days never end, but people end, right?"
My daughter asks me this today. Dazed
by her question, my mind goes blank. I stare.
Then I say, "Yes, people end. All people end
when they're old. It's called death. Days never
end, though, because days are not people

who have blood and bones and skin and..." "Never
mind," she says, going back to the people
in her dollhouse, bending their arms, the right
leg, the left leg, to seat each one in a chair.
But this explanation will not be the end
of it. I know there will be other days,

tomorrow perhaps, when she will take me unaware
with "Why do people end? Will Mommy end?
Will you end? Will I end?" So I'll have to get it right.
I'll have to clear my throat, sigh as wise people
sigh before I say, "Emily, you must never
doubt that God made people end to fill the endless days

in Heaven." Then she'll ask about Heaven, and right
away I'll be in trouble because I'll never
be convincing about a place where people
have wings and play harps, a place without days
and nights, or of just one day without end.
Even if satisfied with that, she'll want to know where

it is and about God and what gives God the right
to make us do anything he pleases, as though people
were dolls and the world a dollhouse. At my wit's end,
I'll probably blurt out something I'll regret for days,
such as, "God's like a person, but we really can't compare
God to a person because God, you know, will never

end as people do." To which she'll say, "So the days
are like God then because the days don't end
either, right Dad?" I will smile in despair.
I will smile and nod and hope she never
asks again. I will watch her play with her people,
watch her bend their wooden heads to the left and the right.

Smoking

I miss the first cigarette of the day,
the one before both eyes are open,
the one before shaving,
the one before showering,
the one before dressing,
the one before breakfast.

I miss the smoke that rises to the ceiling
like mist on a lake in the mountains.
I miss the cigarette after breakfast,
the one with the coffee.
I miss the second cigarette with the coffee.

I miss the cigarette in the car,
my left arm dangling out the window.
I miss guessing how long the ash will hold
before falling off while I'm stopped at a red light.

I miss the cigarette in the men's room.
I miss the hiss of the cigarette butt
as it hits the bowl water.

I miss the cigarettes at lunch
and the round black ashtrays on the table.
I miss the cigarettes at work
and the square glass ashtray on the desk.

I miss my Zippo lighter.
I miss holding it in my hand,
opening and closing it.
I miss the soft click it made when it opened
and the sharp click it made when it snapped shut.
I miss rubbing my Zippo lighter with my thumb.
I miss the real smooth stainless steel feel.
I miss lighting a stranger's cigarette with it on the street.
I miss feeling smooth.
I miss the flawless flame of my Zippo lighter.
I miss saying the word Zippo... Zippo...Zippo.

I miss the last cigarette of the day,
the one just before going to bed,
the one you least enjoy,
the one you don't even know you had.

Banks

In the Chase Manhattan Bank branch
on the corner of 235th Street
and Johnson Avenue, I have changed
my mind about banks. I never used
to like banks. I despised banks. Now
I like banks. I like standing in the cool
lobbies of banks. I like the brass stanchions
and the velvet ropes that are swagged
between them that you must follow
to the tellers' windows, as though through
a maze. I like the ballpoint pens chained
to the counters where you fill out deposit
slips and withdrawal slips. I like the blue
deposit slips and the pink withdrawal slips.
I like the look on the faces of the tellers,
especially when there are many customers
waiting. They are the concentrated faces
of efficiency. I like to say something
pleasant and polite and civil to the tellers
when it is my turn at the window.
Their gratitude is palpable. It shows on
their efficient faces, and I like that.
I like being a number. I like being several
numbers. I never thought I'd like being
a number, but I do. I like being a number
and a face without a name. It is such
a pleasure not having a name for a little
while during the day. How tiring it is
to answer to a name all the time. I like
the air-conditioned, clean smell of banks.
I like the brand new bills they give me.
I like the way they smell and feel and look.
They remind me of the brand new
books they gave me in school, that I was
the first to use. I like the word. I like
the sound of the word "bank." It's the sound
the vault makes when it's shut and locked.
I like to look at the big vault door. I like

the shiny brushed steel of it. I like
the solidity of it, the indestructibility.
I like the enormous tumblers of the locks.
I like the timing mechanism in its glass
case. I like the handle, big as the handle
on the air-lock of a submarine. The door
looks strong enough to keep out death,
master-thief, genius of safe-crackers.
I do not like death.

I Wanted to Know What Poetry Is

I wanted to know what poetry is,
so I looked it up in the dictionary.

Poetry is "expression in poems,"
said the Webster Handy College Dictionary.

I was not happy with this definition,
so I looked it up again.

Poetry is "the art or work of a poet."
That's what I found in The American Heritage Dictionary.

I was not very happy what that one either.
I looked it up a third time.

Poetry, according to Dictionary.com,
is "the art of rhythmical composition,

written or spoken, for exciting pleasure
by beautiful, imaginative, or elevated thoughts."

Now that's more like it, I thought.
But still I was not satisfied, not totally.

I agree that poetry ought to excite
pleasure imaginatively, but I disagree

with the notion that poetry need be
beautiful or elevated to do so.

So I looked it up in the OED.
Poetry, it said, is "literary work

in which special intensity is given
to the expression of feelings and ideas

by the use of distinctive style and rhythm."
Here's what I'm looking for, I thought.

And even though there's no imagination,
it does have special intensity.

Special intensity.
That will do quite well for me.

Yes, that works very well indeed for me,
that intensely special special intensity.

The Schools of Poetry

The first was my elementary school, P.S. 76.
There I learned that poetry
is red roses, blue violets, sweet sugar, and so you are.

The second was my junior high school, Olinville.
There I learned that poetry
is a yellow wood with two diverging roads.

The third was my high school, Evander Childs.
There I learned that poetry
is the dwelling place of possibility.

The fourth was my college, Herbert H. Lehman.
There I learned that poetry
has a favorite month, April the cruelest.

The fifth was my graduate school, State University of New York.
There I learned that poetry
is a cold eye cast on life, on death, of a horseman passing by.

My Grandfather on My Mother's Side

My grandfather on my mother's side had a favorite saying.
Live in the moment is what he said.
So I lived in the moment.

My grandmother on my father's side had a favorite saying.
Live for the moment is what she said.
So I lived for the moment.

One of my uncles had a favorite saying.
Live by the moment is what he said.
So I lived by the moment.

A zen master in a book I read had a favorite saying.
Live as the moment is what he said.
So I lived as the moment.

A zen master in another book I read had a favorite saying.
Live with the moment is what he said.
So I lived with the moment.

My friend Jeff has a favorite saying.
Live without prepositions is what he says.
So I live moments. So moments are what I live.

Next to the Old Mountain Laurel

Next to the old mountain laurel
that is all but dead, there are only three
or four live clusters of leaves left,
and these but barely, I planted another
mountain laurel, young and vigorous,
all living green, free of blemish, not
a dead spot to be found anywhere,
with a future of many years ahead of it.
I did this to make the old mountain man
jealous, jealous enough to keep on going.
Why not? It works with old men sometimes.

Invisible Blue

I built it from the ground up with invisible blue.
At first with shovel and pick, what slow
work that was, I was ground down but made
it stand the test of time, so in time the time
of testing passed. The top of the cherry tree
passed the first sky and the next sky,
and then the last. Do not come down, stay
with the sky, never fall to earth below.
I built it from the ground up with invisible blue.

Late

It is getting late, yes, you know, and perhaps later
than that, but there is no such thing as too late,
especially for the late bloomers, like you,
and most especially for the moon, last
of the late bloomers which is now just arisen
behind you in the garden, one hand for support
on the split rail fence, the other patting you
on the back, "It's all right, son, better late than never."

Corrections

1.

Because I was too lazy to look
it up in the dictionary,
a word in the poem I wrote
on October third was spelled incorrectly.
I am sorry.
The word is anecdote.

2.

A poem I wrote in April
about Shakespeare's King Lear
is based on a premise totally false.
I feel like such a fool.
Please ignore the error.

3.

Two years ago I wrote a poem
about walking on the road at night.
I'm sorry to say I misidentified a star.
Accept my apology, please.
The star is Polaris, not Betelgeuse.

4.

In a poem entitled Going to School,
the comma in the sixth line
of the fourth stanza is out of place.
Forgive my ignorance.
It should be after "golden rule."

5.

I suppose you noticed the word "saliva"
in my poem about the flowers in my garden.
Yeah, you're right.
It should be "salvia."
Damn careless of me.
Sorry. Mea
culpa. What a mess.

6.

Due to the error on the part of the editors of Natural
Bridge, the first line of my poem
entitled "House Ghazal"
contains the word tale.
What a screw-up.
It should be table.
Didn't they see the couplet makes no sense?
Nope.
Inexcusable.

Beautiful Day

It was a beautiful day today.
It was mild. There was a breeze,

firm but gentle. It pushed
the crowns of the trees the way

a father pushes a daughter in a swing.
The rhododendrons were in bloom.

The bees were busy in them.
The peonies were starting to unknot.

The sky was fresh with bright blue.
The clouds were white and soft.

They floated like flowers on the pond
of sky. I heard the song of wrens

as they sang in their house in the beech.
It was beautiful today. My daughter

made beautiful swings in the swing.
My wife made beautiful sounds at the piano.

I thought beautiful things in the chair on the lawn.
It was so beautiful I wanted to scream.

I screamed a long, loud scream.
It had one vowel and no consonants.

Then I screamed a second scream.
Then I screamed a third scream.

Both had one vowel and no consonants.
The telephone rang. It was my neighbor.

He wanted to know if everything was all right.
I said the day was so beautiful I screamed.

He said, Ah, I understand and hung up.
A police car arrived. The officer knocked.

He said he got a report of three loud screams.
I said the day was so beautiful I screamed.

He said, Ah, I understand and drove away.
A fire truck pulled into my driveway.

Three firemen jumped off. They had axes.
They said they got a call about a fire.

I pointed to my heart. It was burning in my chest.
They could see the glow through my skin.

They said, Ah, we understand and left,
leaving me burning and glowing burning and glowing.

PART II

When You Hit the Stones

POEM BASED ON THE LAST LINE OF A POEM BY MYSELF

When you hit the stones,
all you will hear
is the sound of stones hitting.

When you hit the stones,
you should not
blame the stones.

When you hit the stones,
you cannot tell which stone
will remember you longer.

When you hit the stones,
you must explain clearly
what the stones did wrong.

When you hit the stones,
the stones will cry
out in your language.

When you hit the stones,
put them back exactly
where you found them.

When you hit the stones,
the branches of the oaks
will think they are next.

When you hit the stones,
wash your hands in
the first stream to the south.

When you hit the stones,
visualize the center
of the stones.

When you hit the stones,
be prepared, for the moon
will be startled from its sleep.

When you hit the stones,
breathe in the dust you
make from hitting the stones.

When you hit the stones,
reinvent the dance
your ancestors danced.

When you hit the stones,
stop hitting
everything else.

When you hit the stones,
your heart
must already be a stone.

When you hit the stones,
the valley will laugh
at how foolish you are.

Slug

Ugly, sluggish, sluggard, glued-to-the-slab-of-road slug,

you are the length of my little finger,
and you are no thicker at the thickest part
of yourself than the tip of my little finger,
and it will take more luck than exists in the world
for you to reach the other side of the road.

I do not understand how you lug yourself about at all.
It seems to me you ought to be a creature of water,
of rivers, of bays, of lakes.
It seems to me you ought to be stuck fast to something,
to a coral reef in a lagoon, to a rock on a coast full of slugs on rocks.
It seems to me you ought to be sucking plankton into your body
not trying to suck your way across this road.

There is nothing about you I can call beautiful or graceful
or clever.
But perhaps it is beauty and grace and cleverness
that accounts for the ocean inside your body.

Slug.
Even your name has no bones.
Even your name is soft and pliant and glutinous.
Even your name is vulnerable.

If I pick you up, will you remember the pinch in your body?
If I carry you between my thumb and forefinger,
and deposit you in the grass on the other side of the road,
will you remember your journey through the air,
through the air?

**To the Deaf Student in My Poetry Class Before I Play
a Recording of Dylan Thomas**

I don't know what to say.
But don't worry.
I will not assign you the essay the others will have to write.
I don't know what to say.

He was Welsh.
I was hoping that would be all I'd need to say.
But it isn't. I know. Okay.
Let me tell you about his voice.

His voice is a bass-baritone voice.
His voice is a deep, broad, full, bass-baritone voice.
His voice is not thin anywhere.
Can you imagine that?

His voice has no hint of tin in it.
Does that make any sense?
His voice is a deep, broad, full yet clear bell with no tin in it.
His voice is a bass-baritone bell.

His voice is the ringing of the bells of Welsh churches.
Can you imagine that?
His voice is the bells of the churches of Wales,
sometimes sounding births, sometimes deaths,

sometimes sounding weddings, sometimes alarm,
sounding sometimes weather or the sea,
or sometimes only the time of day.
Does any of this make sense?

He was Welsh.
He was a singer.
He died from drinking seventeen straight whiskeys
in a saloon in New York at age 39.

I don't know what to say.
Here are the poems he reads.
Read them to yourself.
Sing them to yourself.

Ring them to yourself.
Become a bell in a Welsh church.
Don't worry.
I will not assign the essay the others will have to write.

Write what you hear.
Be a Welsh church bell.
Sway to and fro in your chair.
Don't worry.

Just write what you hear.
Don't worry.
It will be the best poem in class all year.
It will be better than anything I have to say.

The Author Mural Above the Coffee Bar at Barnes & Noble

Not one is smiling.
Not even Twain.
But it is hard to smile with a big cigar in your mouth.
To Twains's right is Oscar Wilde.
He looks lost and embarrassed.
It has just occurred to him that he is not in the gay bar he
thought he had gone into.
To Twain's left is George Bernard Shaw.
He and Twain are trading witticisms.
They're trying to one-up each other.
But Wilde has already one-upped both of them.
Next to Twain and Shaw, at his own table, Thomas Hardy is
smoking a pipe.
He is leaning over toward them.
He's deciding if he wants to write a comic novel for a change.
He decides he doesn't.
I take it back.
Kafka is smiling.
But he's wearing the wrong hat.
It should be a bowler, not a fedora.
At least it's black, like the suit he always wore, even in summer.
Emily Dickinson and Pablo Neruda share the next table.
This is her first time out in years.
She's dazed.
She's staring off into space.
She's writing a poem on a napkin.
She has already put a pile of napkins in her coat pocket.
At least she's not wearing that white dress.
Neruda wrote her a fan letter.
The sort that Robert Browning wrote to Elizabeth Barrett.
I love your poems and I love you.
He isn't looking at her either.
He's writing a poem in his head.
Something in Spanish about taking off her clothes.
Tagore looks sad.
In fact, Tagore is the saddest one, except for Emily Dickinson.
Nabakov and Joyce are sitting shoulder to shoulder.
They are looking in opposite directions.

But they seem to be sharing an arm.
Next to them, Dorothy Parker is one-upping Oscar Wilde.
But no one's paying any attention to her.
Here's the left profile of a handsome man with blonde hair.
He's paying attention to an attractive woman in a slouch hat.
Neither one is named.
A mistake.
The man is surely F. Scott Fitzgerald, and the woman is certainly Zelda.
I recognize them from photographs.
Then again, perhaps it isn't a mistake.
Perhaps it's the artist's editorial comment.
Or Barnes's comment.
Or Noble's.
At least Fitzgerald's face is there.
Pity poor Hemingway.
There's no trace of him.
And Hawthorne.
And Melville.
And Poe.
Where are they?
But Whitman is here, drinking his cup of leaves of grass herbal tea.
At the last table sit Faulkner, Steinbeck, and Eliot.
Faulkner is smoking a pipe and on his first or third bourbon and soda.
A seltzer bottle is on the table, next to two empty glasses.
Did Steinbeck drink one?
Did Eliot drink one?
Eliot is drinking a cup of coffee.
Steinbeck looks embarrassed.
Way off at the other end of the bar, all by himself, sits Anthony Trollope.
He's writing yet another novel I will never read.

Ode to Coffee

Wine of the bean.
Why do I call you wine of the bean?
I call you by your first name.
I call you by your Arabic name.
I call you what they who first knew you called you.
Those were the Sufi mystics.
Copiously they drank you to keep them awake all night for their all-
night prayers.

Coffe, coffee, coffee.
Three times I lift my cup to you.
With you with you.
Three times you clap your strong black hands in front of me.
Three times squarely in front of my face.
Three times squarely between my half-closed eyelids.

Clap! Clap! Clap!

Morning companion.
Unfailing, faithful friend of my kitchen table.
I look deeply into your black-hearted soul.
I see there my own black-hearted dreams.
The black-hearted nightmares of my nights.
What are they?
They are falling off cliffs.
They are drowning in rivers.
They are being pursued by an assassin without a face.

Coffee, coffee, coffee,
I swallow you three times.
And so I consume the living black hearts of my enemies.
And so I assume the great height of the cliff.
So I assume the awesome power of the river.
So I assume the single-mindedness of the assassin without a face.

Coffee, coffee, coffee.
Now let me not forget that you also have enemies.
You also have nightmares.

You also live in the valley of the shadow of death.
Let me not forget there are those who would becloud you with milk.
There are those who would befog you with cream.
There are those who would bewilder you with half-and-half.
There are those who would befoul you with the sickliness of sugar.
And there are those, even those, who would poison you with the sweet-
ness of chemistry.

These things will I never do.
O companion of my morning!
O faithful unfailing friend of my kitchen table!
O blood-brother wine of the bean!
O comrade coffee!

Pocket Watch

It is one of the most beautiful things
I've ever seen, this pocket watch
in this window of this jewelry store.

It is more beautifully intricate than a spider's
beautifully intricate web. It is more polished
than a stone polished to glossiest gloss

in a stream. Its face is a blue more sublime
than the beautifully sublime blue of the Aegean.
Its hour hand marks the most beautiful hours

of all the hours in the world. Its minute hand
marks the most beautiful minutes of all
the minutes. Its second hand marks

the most beautiful of all the seconds.
Its whispered ticking is a ticking whisper
more seductive than the whisper of lips.

It has a name that sounds like the beautiful name
of the most expensive French champagne.
But the most beautiful thing is that you can do

to time with it what time does to you.
You can carry it around in your pocket
all day long, and, from time to time, look at it.

The Frog

It was a beautiful summer evening in Edo.
I think it was 1686.
But I could be wrong.
Maybe it was 1687.
Any way, I was sitting on my favorite lily pad,
just as I always do at dusk.
The wind had died down.
The air was still.
As was the water of the pond still, very still.
The stars were just beginning to wake up from
their sleep under the golden blanket of the sun.
I was singing my favorite song,
the one I learned as a tadpole,
the song about the moon,
that bright lily on the dark lily pad of night,
when suddenly,
I heard the rustle of a reed,
the split of a stick.
Of course, I took no chances.
Bash!
Oh, head first into the pond!

To My Beard

What can I say but I am sorry,
I apologize for what I do to you,
my daily ruthlessness and cruelty.
What can I do but ask for your forgiveness
and your patience. For someday,
I promise you, someday I swear
on the beards of the prophets,
and on the beard of the poet Whitman,
and on the beard of the president Lincoln,
and on the red beard of the grandfather,
I will not stop you any longer,
I will let you go free, I will take down
the fence around you made of sharp blades.
For someday, I promise you, I will let
you run wild through the valleys
of my face like a stallion, I will let you
wander over the desert of my face
like a holy man in his vision of heaven
and hell, I will let you grow, blossom
and flourish, and I will stroke you
and comb you and keep you orderly
and free of knots and tangles,
and you in turn will make me look
distinguished, a wise old man as I stroke
you looking serious, looking as though
I were thinking deep thoughts about
life and death. But I will be thinking
only about you, my beard, my second
face, and this will be our secret.

To My Thumbs

So is it you then who
are responsible for me?

Am I all thumbs, after all?
You apposite opposites,

you opposables, do you really
believe you are so indisposable?

Don't be so smug.
Don't be so cocksure of yourselves.

Thumbs down, thumbs.
Screw you.

I know of at least one who
could have written this with his left foot.

And of another one who
could have done it with his teeth.

To My Feet

Sit up here, feet.
Get a load off.

Come up here on the desk,
across from me at legs' length,

so I can see you,
so I can thank you properly.

I want to thank you properly for
taking me everywhere I have needed to go:

Up the steps of libraries
and down the steps of basement restaurants.

Across the avenues of cities and
across the streets of small towns.

Along the hallways of hospitals
and along the corridors of schools.

On the paths of gardens, the trails of forests,
the sands of beaches, the grass of meadows,

the polished floors of gymnasiums.
Sit up here, feet.

How tired you look.
How weary you must be from carrying me

around on your shoulders all these years.
Rest a while, feet.

Soon enough will people
begin to whisper, hiding their mouths

behind their hands, that I look like
I have one of you in the grave.

To My Eyes

Runts of the litter, you
were always the weakest ones.
You were always the neediest.
Right from the start,
in first grade, my mother had
to get those heavy glass
crutches for you. How stupid
you looked walking around
with them. How embarrassed
you were. How helpless
you were without them. That
was what the bullies went for first.
How they loved to kick the glass
crutches out from under you
and laugh as you froze in place.
And the eye doctors were wrong,
the ones who said you would
improve, who said that someday
you would not need them anymore.
They are lighter now, it's true,
less bulky, more stylish. And
even though you need them
more than ever, all in all, things
could have been worse. You
have become such talented
historians. See how much more
I have learned from the two of
you than I could have learned
from a hundred history books,
for you have showed me so vividly,
so true-to-life what life was like
a thousand years ago, as I walk
the rough roads, my hand on
the shoulder of my daughter or
my son, who curses me as I stumble.

To My Favorite Corduroy Jacket

Such dust on your shoulders.
How did you get such dust
on your shoulders? Have you
been holding up the ceiling of
the closet all summer? I see
you are getting old. I see how
thin you are getting. Soon
I will have to replace
the leather patches where
my elbows have worn you
through. And your satin
lining. What a mess. You
can't even hold a pen in
your inside pocket anymore.
It just falls through to the floor.
Your lapels, which when I first
set eyes on them, I thought
were the wings of Pegasus,
are gnarled, curled, useless
as the wings of an ostrich.
At least you have all your
buttons. You're lucky,
although it's true, one's life
is hanging by a thread.
How ironic that is since
except for that one time
when I first tried you on,
I've never buttoned you up.
I wonder why. Could it be
I am so shy, timid, uncertain
of my own mind that I always
let you speak for me?
I must remember to tell
the undertaker to button your
lip along with mine. I know
I should send you away
to the tailor to be sewn,
but I'm afraid to send you

away. I also am getting old,
and I'm afraid to be apart
from you, even for just a week.
Haven't I already sworn (Do
you remember?) that I will
die in your arms -- O corduroy
armor – O corduroy critic-proof
vest – that we will become dust
together, that together we will
become dust of corduroy,
dust of man, that we will
become dust of corduroy-man,
and together hold up
the ceiling of the closet of
the earth all summer, all fall,
all winter, all spring?

Horse Ghazal

God created many animals in the Garden of Eden.
Adam's favorite was the dog; Eve's was the horse.

My uncle liked enigmatic expressions.
The best was I need to see a man about a horse.

One of the slang words for heroin is horse.
A bad dream is named for a female horse.

In the Bible, it was lowly to sit upon an ass.
That's why a king would sit upon a horse.

King Solomon imported them from Egypt in great numbers.
He paid 150 shekels of silver for each horse.

The poet must be one with the rhythm of the poem.
Just as the rider must be one with the motion of the horse.

So, Solonche, any last words to offer on this?
It's just another cart before another color of horse.

Cow Ghazal

"The female of the bull" is how
Samuel Johnson defined the cow.

In Norse mythology, Ymir, father of the Giants, was fed
four streams of milk by Audumla the cow.

In Hindu belief, the feminine aspect of Brahma
is known as the "melodious cow."

In the Bible, Yaweh demanded red,
but the pagan sacrifice wanted a white cow.

In Egypt, the goddess Isis was often depicted
wearing the head and horns of a cow.

There was an old man, and he had an old cow.
And over the moon jumped the cow.

So, Solonche, is there a moral to this ghazal?
Yes. Take a deep breath. Relax. Don't have a cow.

Wine Ghazal

The last word in my dictionary is zymurgy.
It is the chemistry of the fermentation of beer or wine.

Hey Omar, who needs a loaf of bread? A book of verse?
All we need, brother, is a full moon and a full flask of wine.

Sometimes I want to think a clear thought and write a clear line.
Sometimes I choose the clearest of clear white wine.

Sometimes I want to sleep a deep sleep and dream a deep dream.
Sometimes I choose the deepest of deep red wine.

I will tell you what the best wine poem in the world is.
It is Pablo Neruda's glorious Ode to Wine.

For instance, taste this: I like on the table, when
we're speaking, the light of a bottle of intelligent wine.

So, Solonche, is there any more on the subject to be said?
Only red to white, all right, and white to red, you're dead.

Glass Ghazal

Of all the books I read as a child, my favorites
were Alice in Wonderland and Through the Looking-Glass.

We were astonished at walking away with only a scratch.
Everywhere inside the car and out was broken glass.

Never mind glasshouse people and their forbidden stones.
People who live in stone houses shouldn't throw glass.

Emily Dickinson wrote more than seventeen-hundred poems.
Only one begins with the word glass.

The antique purple brooch said my mother was amethyst.
Years later, the jeweler shrugged and said, Glass.

My daughter says a looking-glass is a window,
not a mirror, which is a looking-at-yourself-glass.

So, Solonche, what is it you really want to say?
Ah, your question is a diamond; my answer is glass.

Sky Ghazal

The first color of the sky is blue.
Invisible blue is the last color of the sky.

Which is the wiser, the lion or the eagle?
The eagle is, for the lion knows nothing of the sky.

With a clear night sky, you will see millions of stars.
And every one has its own clear night sky.

Because Lucifer and his angels were rebellious, they were expelled.
As they fell to earth, they took their last deep breath of sky.

The poet said, "Do not bury me in the ground."
The poet said, "Bury me in the sky."

The beginning of the world was water.
The end of the world will be the sky.

So, Solonche, are you quite satisfied?
Yes. Enough of this mile-wide pie-in-the-sky.

House Ghazal

My daughter asks, "Is Sleeping Beauty a fairy table?"
"No," I say. "But it is the most important thing in a fairy's house."

Although it must have other things to do, winter will not leave.
I'm tired of brown and gray, and I'm tired of the house.

Someday I'll build the poem of my dreams.
It will be too big, too grand, a folly, like every dream-house.

My wife sits down to play Chopin on the piano.
She opens the door to her own black and white house.

Does one really need to see who one is and when?
Does one really need twelve mirrors and eight clocks in one's house?

Although I've been calling a week, spring does not answer.
Right now a woodpecker dials from a tree in front of the house.

So, Solonche, how long will you go on this way?
Not long. The wise man knows it's best to make silence his house.

To the Rabbit I Killed on the Road This Morning

When I am dead as you are dead,
struck down by cancer cells rampaging
in my bladder or my pancreas,
in my lymph nodes or my bones or both,
or by my left anterior descending coronary
artery strangling my heart to death,
or by a driver driving too fast, too
carelessly on a narrow country road to see
me in time to swerve away, and if
my spirit should meet your spirit,
I tell you now it will submit.
My spirit will do anything yours will
ask of it to satisfy what justice might
be there in such a place of mingled
spirits. Except one thing. One thing
your spirit must not ask of mine,
even if it is the only price it must exact.
My spirit must refuse to change
places with your spirit. My spirit
must forever be that of homo sapiens
sapiens, as yours must be forever
that of sylvilagus cuniculus,
and this will not be my human hubris
but rather its greater punishment,
my wise spirit forever thinking
about your wedge-toothed, forest-
dwelling spirit. To forever envy it.

Beauty

From my room down the hall,
I can hear the mathematics
professor getting emotional
about an equation, and I ask
myself how someone can get
so worked up about what isn't real,
an abstraction, nothing but
signs and symbols. A scribble.

Oh, I say to myself. To him
it is a poem, a formal one,
every word in place, every rhyme
perfect, every stanza exact. Poor man.
He, too, must pound the beauty in
with his fist. Every time. Every damn time.

E Equals Em Cee Squared

Energy is the same as mass
multiplied by the speed

of light (celeritas,
swiftness in Latin)

multiplied
by itself. See?

As I've been
saying for years,

everything becomes clear
when everything becomes poetry.

Five-time Pushcart Prize nominee as well as Best of the Net nominee, J.R. Solonche has been publishing poetry in magazines, journals, and anthologies since the early 70s. Among the 300 or so print and on-line publications in which his work has appeared are *The American Scholar, The New Criterion, The Journal of the American Medical Association, Poetry Northwest, The Progressive, The North American Review, Poet Lore, Poetry East, Rattle, Barrow Street, The Hampden-Sydney Poetry Review, The Atlanta Review, Salmagundi, Yankee Magazine, The Literary Review, Natural Bridge, Nimrod, Fugue, the Anthology of Magazine Verse & Yearbook of American Poetry, Visiting Frost: Poems Inspired by the Life and Work of Robert Frost, Mixed Voices: Contemporary Poems about Music, Facing the Change: Personal Encounters with Global Warming, Dogs Singing: A Tribute Anthology,* and *A Ritual to Read Together: Poems in Conversation with William Stafford.*

Professor Emeritus of English at the State University of New York-Orange County, author of *Won't Be Long (*Deerbrook Editions 2016*), Heart's Content, Invisible, and The Black Birch,* and he is coauthor (with his wife Joan I. Siegel) of *Peach Girl: Poems for a Chinese Daughter.*